Clouds:
On the Wind

Poems for the Soul -
A Meditation

Gary W. Burns

WWW.TURNINGCORNERBOOKS.COM

Copyright © 2013 by Vista View Publishing

Published by:
Turning Corner Books
PO Box 121
Haymarket, VA 20168

All rights reserved under International
And Pan-American Copyright Conventions.

Library of Congress Control Number: 2010930365
ISBN: 978-0-9845342-0-3

Forth Printing, May 2018

Designed, inclusive of all artwork by Gary W. Burns
(with the exception of jacket artwork)

Jacket Artwork: Wheat Field with Cypresses, Vincent van Gogh;
Metropolitan Museum of Art, NY, NY: faithful photographic
reproduction, public domain; Wikimedia Commons

No part of this book may be reproduced in any form without
permission in writing from the publisher; except by a reviewer,
who may quote brief passages in a review to be printed in a
magazine, newspaper or posted to the World Wide Web.
Particular emphasis is laid on the matter of broadcasting,
recording and public performance.

Other Books of Poetry by Gary W. Burns

Bridges: To There
(Poems for the Mind, Body & Spirit)

Dawn and Beyond: Embark
(Poetry – Come Destiny)

Earth Tones: A Journey
(Poetry for the Journey)

Garden Walks: Hand In Hand
(Poems To Relax By)

Moments: This to the Next
(Poetry - Now and Eternity)

Poems of Love: A Selection Vol. I

Poems of Love: A Selection Vol. II

Rainy Day: Wondering
(Poems for a Rainy Day)

Twilight: Awaking the Stars
(Poems of the Night's Light)

*To Debra
For Her Loving Spirit*

ॐ ———————

Contents

Clouds Moonlit

Quietly There You Be	17
Minstrels All	18
Light Dancer	19
From the Very Beginning	20
The Embrace	21
Night Clouds	22
Nevertheless	23
On the Wind	24
As Eternal Is	25
At Peace	26
Meditation I	27
Of You and Me	28
The Grandeur of Night	29
In Rhapsody	30
Doorway	31

Cloudy Day Doorway

Embark	35
Still We Danced	36
Meditation II	37
Places	38
Crossroads	39
Quiet Does	40
Sun and Moon	41
Leaving	42
To You	44
Our Way	45
Let's Do	46
So Very Good	47
Towering	48
Only You Will Know	49
Blue Ridge Twilight	50
To Tranquility	52
Of Love	53
Soul Serenade	54
By the Hearth	55

Windswept

Blue Sky	59
Ever As Dear	60
Timelessness	61
And Know Them	62
The Passage To	63
Paradox Untangled	64
All In All	65
Smile	66
This Day	67
Beckon Bright	68
Forgive	69
Not Now	70
Meditation III	71
Harmony	
In Clouds: On the Wind	72
Who Could Argue That	73
Winds of Change	74
Pathless Odyssey	75

Wind Songs

O Mystery	79
More	80
Days With You	81
The Jeweled Crown	82
Solution	83
Misty	84
Meditation IV	85
Joyful	86
9:00 AM	87
Beauty Sketched	88
Umbrella	89
Patterns	90
Dispel	91
To Comfort	92
Perception	93
My Friend	94
Any Song	95
Inevitably	96
Calm	97
Mindfulness	98
Essence	99

Clouds Moonlit

Quietly There You Be

There's a quiet place
It's not too far from where you are

To get there
There are

No corners to turn
Nor a step to go up
Nor a step to go down
Nor a wall to go round

You see
It's the discovery

Of Be -

There's a quiet place
It's not too far
From where you are

Quietly

There
You
Be

Minstrels All

*Stardust
Springs
In Earthly things*

*Melodiously
The heart sings*

Minstrels all

Light Dancer

Dance on
Light dancer
Dance on

Dance

With the love that holds
The moon and the stars
Dancing through
Mystic hours

Dance on
Light dancer
Dance on

From
The Very Beginning

From
The very beginning
I gave
My heart to you

But then,
Of course
You knew

For, it was you
Who my heart
First belonged to

Love

The Embrace

Warmth flowing,
Soul whirling,
Eyes wondrous

Embracing

Love

Night Clouds

Night clouds
Ride stars
Through galaxies

Each
An infinity

Each a you
And each a me

Nevertheless

We can't see the breeze,
We can't see our souls;

Nevertheless.

On the Wind

Seeing
A nebulous flock
Of birds
Fleet by,
Wing on wind,

Then again,

Seeing a lone bird
Winging the wind,
People and life
Come to thought.

Many stories
One wind.

As Eternal Is

As eternal is
The bright of light

It is
The dark of night

At Peace

*Nothing
To go to*

*Nothing
To come from*

*Be
At peace*

In One

Meditation I

Peaceful
Be

Tranquil
Me

Of You And Me

Night,
Showering star-drops
Eternally

Rains
Eternity

You and me

The Grandeur Of Night

As tender night, wept
In joy
And ebony teardrops fell

The beauty of the moon
Shined through
The lacey teardrop veil:

O the grandeur
Of the night

In Rhapsody

*Cloaked
By the stars,
And harbored
By the break of day*

*Night
Steals away
As we sway*

In the rhapsody

Of Love.

Doorway

Born
Ever new from night
Morning's gray-dappled light

Whispers
Endlessly

'Starlight
Sleep tight'.

Cloudy Day Doorway

Embark

So many things
Are taken away

One might wonder
Where's the giving

Living

Embark

Still We Dance

1
While the Earth
Creatively
Sang a song
For you and me

The sky spoke
Solemnly,
"Rain".
And
We danced
To music eternal.

2
Some call it Cosmic,
Some call it Earthly,
Some call it Simply
You
And
Me.

3
O still
We dance.

Meditation II

The wind
 Rustling the leaves:
 Us
 In the breeze.

Places

Alighting
Amid cattails
Amassed
Alongside the pond
A red winged blackbird,
Articulating its song,
Found a place to be.

And here,
Amid the dark of night
And the light of day

We as well
Have found
A place to stay

For awhile,
Anyway.

Crossroads

Every world
Is as real,

Your world
Or mine.

Crossroads.

Quiet Does

Quiet does
What quiet should

Understood
A doorway to good

Enter
And
Be

Peacefully

Sun and Moon

Give light not a crown
Nor dark a prince:
Birth is the gift of sight
And death a birthright

Harmony

Leaving

1
Today's autumn wind,
Breathing motion
Into rocking tree and limb,
Blows
And windrows
Leaves
Of yellow, red,
Brown
And gold.

Windy days
Are surely made
To take leaves from trees.

When the time's right
Leaves
Leave the only home,
As leaves,
They've ever known.

2
Some say of the leaving
It's the great cycle,
Others say of it,
It's
Just a change of season,
There's no other reason.

But, whatever the reason,
Season blends into season
And leaves
Leave the trees
And the only home,
As leaves,
They've ever known.

To You

Storms like rain
Stars like night hours

Seas like the tint of blue
And the Soul likes
A warmth that's true

Be true
To you

Our Way

Sometimes
We get lost

And that's okay
Life's a mystery
As we go
Our Way

Let's Do

Will you

Think of me my Friend

Every now and then

And

Now and again

I will think of you

My life through

Let's do

So Very Good

*The pace of a busy day
May be hard to ease away;*

*But, ease away you should,
For the restfulness
Is so very
Very good.*

Towering

Towering
Not over
But among;

Love.

Only You Will Know

Some things will never come
Some things will never go

Choices,
Perhaps not
Perhaps so

Only you will know

Blue Ridge Twilight

1
From atop this mountain
One can see
Autumn's calico woods
Playfully

Chasing

The long river ribbon
Running along
Twilight banks.

2
Quickly
Twilight
Tucks itself in

And stars

In black attire

Crown the very ground
Once lit bright
By autumn sunlight.

3
Then, with twilight gone,
Once more,
As the night before,
The Blue Ridge Mountains
Sleep deep.

To Tranquility

Move

*In accord
With silence,*

Quietly

*To
Tranquility.*

Of Love

Infinitesimal;
Infinite . . .

Soul Serenade

At quiet times
All rhythms
Rhyme.

By the Hearth

It's cold outside.

There's snow
On the ground.

It's warm
Inside,

Here,

By the hearth
Of the soul.

Feel love

And warm

By the hearth
Of the soul.

Windswept

Blue Sky

1
How wondrous
The blue sky
With windswept clouds
High.

2
Dear clouds on blue
Write for us
Your poetry
Sing for us
Your song.

3
O how we long
To be
Windswept with you
In sky blue beauty too.

Ever As Dear

The sun
Forever embraces its light
The moon
Holds tight the night

Our Souls
Are ever as dear
Don't fear

Come near

Timelessness

*Let timelessness
Exist*

*And in the peacefulness
You come to know*

Grow

And Know Them

May bliss
Be
Your life long companion

May happiness
Be
Your closest friend

Love

And know them

The Passage To

I hope for you
A quiet moment
Opens up

And you move through
The passage to

Boundless
Peace;

It awaits you
Move through

Paradox Untangled

*Have your heart
In mind*

All In All

For these brief moments
Of time
You give me heartbeats
Of love

For all else
Love boundless

Smile

Calm the flurry
Of your hurried soul

Sail
The wonderful sea
Of a smile

This Day

Earth
Destiny willed

And sky
Cloud filled

Say
'This day
Is the Way'

Beckon Bright

Love,
Beckon bright,
Guiding with delight

Holds
Tight

The meek
And the bold
Alike.

Forgive

Love
Forever
Gives

Feel

Love
And heal

Not Now

What point of departure
Is not
Now...?

Meditation III

*Now will be tomorrow
As it was yesterday*

*Be
Today*

*Let now
Be your way*

Harmony

The rising and falling
Of the breast

The air
In

The air
Out:

Clouds
Sail the wind

> *In Clouds: On the Wind*

Who Could Argue That

Our time together,
Short though it was,
Was
And who
Could argue that

But, you should know

We'll never truly part

For, how can one part
From the beat of One Heart

Winds of Change

The winds have changed
And brought
A need to rearrange

The way
I thought the day
Would move along

Still
I am my song

Sung
The day long

Pathless Odyssey

*It's your venture
Venture on*

Free

*Free
To
Be*

*Your
Pathless
Odyssey*

Wind Songs

O Mystery

O mystery
Light for me
A fire
That I may see
My home
Eternity.

I'll let go

Of whatever
I Believe
I know.

O mystery
Light for me
A fire
That I may see
My home
Eternity.

More

You are more
Than the dark
Of night
Or the light
Giving
Daylight
Sight

Celebrate

You are more

Days With You

I've seen them
As great birds
In flight

And rainbow-like
At sunset
Glowing bright,

The amorphous clouds.

It's on these days
With you
They turn into
Butterflies
And hummingbirds too.

The Jeweled Crown

Sad at loss

Happy at found;

Love,

The jeweled crown.

Solution

Love all things;

*The heart
In harmony*

Sings.

Misty

At first

Misty
The view

Then with
Gentle thoughts

Mist clears
Soul appears

Harmony
Nears

Meditation IV

Dear Eternity

> *Teach me*
> *To ever present*
>
> > *Be*
>
> *And to know*
> *You are everywhere*
> > *I go*

Joyful

Looking forward,
Thinking back

But,
Being

Just where you are;

Joyful.

9:00 AM

9:00 AM
Tranquil

Sun by moon

Clouds
In tune

Beauty Sketched

Beauty,
Sketched:

Stillness

Umbrella

An umbrella for the soul

Caring

Patterns

In the heat
Of a hot day
One might say,

'If only
It would cloud up
And give
Some cooling rain,
O if only'.

Then clouds cloud up
And rains come down
Then
One wishes again
For the sun to come round.

O the glad to sad
And the sad to glad;
I guess

It's here to stay

This way
Then that way.

Dispel

Beyond
Within
Is all of without

Beyond
Without
Is all of within

Be within
Be without

Dispel
Doubt

To Comfort

Asked

Hold

Perception

*There's more
Than perception
Could
Ever hope for.*

*But,
As awe slips away
Perception seeks
What it may.*

My Friend

Be patient
And go slowly My Friend.

Let
Whatever goes on around you
Go around you.

The wind blows
Gusts
And gentle breezes.

All things be.

Be patient
And gentle with 'you'
My Friend.

Go slowly.

Any Song

Any song
I chant
I grant
To you.

For, of course,
It's your voice
That makes the choice
Of what rings true.

Inevitably

Listening
To the river run
On splashing feet;
All steps
Taken
At once.

The
Inevitable
Moving towards
Inevitability... ?

And we,
Inevitably ...

Calm

*Know the peace in quiet
As you know your name*

Become the same

Mindfulness

Love
Gave away

What's thought to be
A mystery

Now
Within me

You Be

Harmoniously

Essence

I cannot see
By what light
Essences writes

So,

I ask

The light of the sun,
The halo
Of everyone,
To reflect for me
What I cannot see

About the Author

Inspired by nature and the beauty around him Gary W. Burns started writing poetry at a young age. Early on Gary was able to express his thoughts, ideas and emotions through the vivid imagery of his verse. His poetry has been published in various literary arts journals, anthologies and magazines. He is the author of 10 books of poetry. Through his poems Gary shares his reflections on the many facets of life and on the beauty of nature. The expressiveness of his poetry has been enriched by his wide reading in philosophy and psychology. He has traveled throughout the world and has lived in numerous countries, to include, Italy, Korea, Saudi Arabia and Canada. He has also lived in Hawaii and several other states. Currently, Gary makes his home in Northern Virginia near the foothills of the Blue Ridge Mountains.

ENJOY THESE OTHER BOOKS OF POETRY BY GARY W. BURNS

Moments: This to the Next
(Poetry - Now and Eternity)
ISBN: 978-0-9845342-4-1 (Paperback)
ISBN: 978-0-9827805-1-0 (Hardcover)
ISBN: 978-0-9860900-9-7 (E-Book)

Bridges: To There
(Poems for the Mind, Body & Spirit)
ISBN: 978-0-9827805-6-5 (Paperback)
ISBN: 978-0-9827805-7-2 (Hardcover)
ISBN: 978-0-9860900-4-2 (E-Book)

Earth Tones: A Journey
(Poetry for the Journey)
ISBN: 978-0-9845342-6-5 (Paperback)
ISBN: 978-0-9845342-9-6 (Hardcover)
ISBN: 978-0-9860900-8-0 (E-Book)

Available at WWW.TURNINGCORNERBOOKS.COM and where books are sold.

Dawn and Beyond: Embark
(Poetry - Come Destiny)
ISBN: 978-0-9827805-8-9 (Paperback)
ISBN: 978-0-9827805-9-6 (Hardcover)
ISBN: 978-0-9860900-0-4 (E-Book)

Garden Walks: Hand In Hands
(Poems to Relax By)
ISBN: 978-0-9845342-3-4 (Paperback)
ISBN: 978-0-9827805-0-3 (Hardcover)
ISBN: 978-0-9860900-1-1 (E-Book)

Rainy Day: Wondering
(Poems for a Rainy Day)
ISBN: 978-0-9845342-5-8 (Paperback)
ISBN: 978-0-9827805-2-7 (Hardcover)
ISBN: 978-0-9860900-7-3 (E-Book)

Available at WWW.TURNINGCORNERBOOKS.COM and where books are sold.

Poems of Love: Selection Vol. II
ISBN: 979-8-9909248-0-2 (Paperback)
ISBN: 979-8-9909248-1-9 (Hardcover)
ISBN: 979-8-9909248-2-6 (E-Book)

Twilight: Awaking the Stars
(Poems of the Night's Light)
ISBN: 978-0-9845342-7-2 (Paperback)
ISBN: 978-0-9827805-4-1 (Hardcover)
ISBN: 978-0-9860900-6-6 (E-Book)

Poems of Love: A Selection Vol. I
ISBN: 978-0-9845342-8-9 (Paperback)
ISBN: 978-0-9827805-5-8 (Hardcover)
ISBN: 978-0-9860900-5-9 (E-Book)

Available at WWW.TURNINGCORNERBOOKS.COM and where books are sold.

www.ingramcontent.com/pod-product-compliance
Lightning Source LLC
Chambersburg PA
CBHW051456290426
44109CB00016B/1775